YORKSHIRE DALES IN WINTER

KEITH WOOD

HALSGROVE

First published in Great Britain in 2010

Copyright © Keith Wood 2010

British Library Cataloguing-in-Publication Data
A CIP record for this title is available from the British Library

ISBN 978 0 85704 053 4

HALSGROVE
Halsgrove House,
Ryelands Industrial Estate,
Bagley Road, Wellington, Somerset TA21 9PZ
Tel: 01823 653777   Fax: 01823 216796
email: sales@halsgrove.com

Part of the Halsgrove group of companies
Information on all Halsgrove titles is available at: www.halsgrove.com

Printed and bound by Grafiche Flaminia, Italy

Introduction

THE YORKSHIRE DALES situated high in the Pennines are renowned for their green pastures, drystone walls, field barns, limestone scars and easy walking and are a popular destination in the summer months for visitors of all ages. But as the nights draw in, traffic from visitors diminishes and the Dales are left for the locals apart from a few well publicised seasonal festivals.

In taking on this project I had two main concerns: firstly would there be enough snow and frosty days over the course of a single winter to make a worthwhile collection and secondly if there was snow would I actually be able to get into the Dales travelling from home given the narrow roads and high level passes. The first proved to be totally without foundation as the winter became the worst for 30 odd years with days of snowfall, followed by weeks of freezing cold putting back the arrival of spring by virtually a month compared to recent years. My second concern had some validity as Swaledale proved to be virtually inaccessible after the heavy snow in late December and January and Wharfedale proved equally problematic. Fortunately Wensleydale with its wider roads and better winter maintenance by the gritting crews was accessible, although it will be difficult to forget driving along the snow covered A684 from the Moorcock Inn to Hawes on the morning of the first main snowfall in December, seemingly tip-toeing along in my two wheel drive vehicle. Other days I was forced to turn back or change my route as I reached deep snow or ice-covered roads. However with care and perseverance I was able to gain access to all the major dales and viewpoints.

Having spent the previous summer exploring the Dales, researching some 30 walking routes for a series of walking guides, I thought that I had come to know the area pretty well and had a reasonable plan of the images I wanted to take. However under a blanket of snow the Dales take on a different character. Scenes that worked well in the summer proved less interesting under snow but many more new opportunities presented themselves and I found myself seeing the landscape from an entirely new perspective seeking details as well as sweeping landscapes.

Each dale has its unique flavour from Swaledale in the north with its lead mining heritage, to Wensleydale's wider, more pastoral character, Wharfedale's picturesque villages, and the dales bordering the south of the National Park with limestone scars in abundance. But what they all have in common are drystone walls, field barns, sheep and an astonishing variety of waterfalls. I hope that I have been able to do justice to them all!

Photographing the Dales in winter has been a joyous (and occasionally dangerous) challenge. Even clad in winter clothing, there were times standing in a biting wind waiting for the light, that I longed to get back into the warmth of the car. I hope that you get as much pleasure from looking at this collection of images as I have had in photographing this particular Yorkshire Dales winter's tale.

A sheep shares the view of the early autumn mist along central Wharfedale from Top Mere Road above Kettlewell.

As the summer gives way to autumn, clouds gather above the gateway to Cogden Moor leading to Grinton Smelt Mill in Swaledale.

First hints of autumn colour reflected in the slow moving waters of the River Wharfe taken from the Daleway footbridge near Starbotton.

Autumn colours alongside the Wharfe beside Grass Wood near Grassington – look out for the heron on the left bank.

Weir on the Wharfe below Grassington – the weir and adjacent derelict building just upstream from Linton Falls are actually the remains of a 1920s' hydroelectric power system. The first power house on the site was built by the Grassington Electric Supply Company formed in 1909 to provide an electricity supply to the area.

Weir above Linton Falls – this second weir seen from the footbridge over the Wharfe was originally constructed to provide a water supply to the Linton textile mill.

The picturesque ruins of Bolton Abbey, Wharfedale.

Bolton Abbey was founded in 1155 by the Augustinian order of monks, known as the Black Canons, because of the colour of the robes that they wore. In the priory's heyday of the fourteenth century there were 26 canons and some 200 lay workers. Today the ruins are part of the Yorkshire estate of the Duke of Devonshire. A couple of miles upstream the Wharfe narrows as it gushes through The Strid.

The Wharfe flowing through the
Bolton Abbey Estate.

Looking down onto The Strid from the
viewpoint of Harrison's Ford Seat.

The Wharfe rushes through The Strid at Bolton Abbey.

Bridge over the Wharfe at Bolton Abbey.

The view across Wharfedale from Edge Lane above Grassington on a still early winter's afternoon.

Scale Haw Falls above Hebden, Wharfedale. It's easy to miss these falls in Hebden Gill as they are tucked away at the bottom of a meadow on the track from Hebden to Hole Bottom.

Late afternoon sunshine illuminates the Ribblehead Viaduct.

The 24 arches of the Ribblehead Viaduct which was completed in 1874, carry trains on the famous Settle to Carlisle railway line. Spanning some 440 yards (400m) it is overlooked to the north by Whernside one of the Yorkshire Three Peaks.

The Grassington Dickensian Christmas Festival has established itself over the last 30 years as the Dales' major Christmas event. Held on the three Saturdays leading up to Christmas, each year thousands of visitors pack into the narrow village streets and Market Square to enjoy a variety of traditional festive street entertainments and stalls with local produce.

Above: A flaming brazier to warm visitors in the Market Square.

Top left: Grassington Town Crier prepares to welcome visitors to the town's famous Dickensian Christmas Festival.

Left: Preparing hot nuts to keep out the winter's chill.

Opposite: Leeds Morris Men dancing jigs with a Victorian flavour.

The Penny Plain Theatre Company performing a traditional Mummers' Play at the Grassington Dickensian Christmas Festival.

Opposite: Fire juggler entertaining the crowds.

Wain Wath Force the first of the series of waterfalls around the hamlet of Keld, Upper Swaledale.

Waterfall hunters will delight in the hamlet of Keld, Upper Swaledale. In just over a mile the Swale pours over three sets of falls together with the twin falls of the tributary of East Gill. First comes Wain Wath Force, easily accessible from the road with roadside parking. Next comes Catrake Force which is hidden in a deep gorge immediately below the hamlet and is almost inaccessible for mere mortals. Finally the Swale crashes over Kisdon Force involving a minor scramble in winter conditions. The twin falls of the tributary East Gill are my favourite, easily reached along the Pennine Way footpath out of Keld.

Top: Lower East Gill Falls.

Above: The top of the almost inaccessible Catrake Force below Keld.

Right: Upper East Gill Falls.

First snow of the winter covers Cotter Side, Upper Wensleydale.

Snow clings to the fir trees of Cobbles Plantation,
near Garsdale Head, Upper Wensleydale.

Snow covers the A684 at the Moorcock Inn, Upper Wensleydale.

The Settle to Carlisle Railway travels over the twelve arches of Dandrymire Viaduct just outside Garsdale Station at Garsdale Head.

Looking across to Wild Boar Fell just outside the National Park from Upper Wensleydale.

Snow drifts against drystone walls beside the road near the Moorcock Inn.

Widdale Fell in the distance across Cotterdale Beck.

Having slithered my way along the roller coaster of the A684 from Garsdale Head, just before reaching the entrance to Cotterdale I could not resist stopping to capture this framed image through the farm gates looking towards Widdale Fell.

Trees cast shadows from the early morning sun across fresh snow in the fields beside Cotterdale Beck on the way to Cotter Force.

Opposite: Snow-covered Cotter Force.

A winter wonderland around
Cotterdale Beck.

Deep snow surrounds a field barn in Cotterdale.

Widdale Fell across snow-covered fields from near Appersett, Wensleydale.

Sheep looking for food after the first snow of winter in Cotterdale.

Field barn on the tree-topped Band Rigg, Wensleydale.

I couldn't resist taking this image of a perfect boot print in the fresh snow.

Snow covers the Shepherd statue
in front of the Doctor's Surgery
in the middle of Hawes.

Morning sun illuminates a typical Dales field barn just outside Hawes along Wensleydale.

Deep snow covers the meadows in Wensleydale.

Looking east along a snow-covered Wensleydale.

Central Wensleydale between Hawes and Bainbridge with Abbotside Common in the background.

Above: St Oswald's Church, Askrigg.

Right: Looking across to Askrigg from Bainbridge.

The raised mound of Virosidvm Roman Fort at Bainbridge provided a perfect platform for the next few images looking across to Askrigg and down onto Bainbridge itself. The 2 acre site named VIROSIDVM or "the settlement of true men" is believed to have been founded around 71AD and was deep in territory held by the Brigantes. On my visit it was deep in snow, almost thigh deep on the way up to the flat and wind-blown top.

The view along Wensleydale from the site of Virosidvm Roman Fort at Bainbridge.

Looking down onto the snow-covered village green at Bainbridge.

Falls on the River Bain at Bainbridge of course!

Sunshine illuminates the snow on Abbotside Common, Wensleydale.

The River Ure meanders along central Wensleydale.

Trees crown the top of Lady Hill between Bainbridge and Aysgarth.

Sheep make trails in the snow as they forage for food.

Opposite: Snow drifts against drystone walls in Wensleydale.

Looking down onto St Andrew's Church, Aysgarth.

Bolton Castle dominates the scene in central Wensleydale.

Snow drifts across the A684 between Bainbridge and Hawes – I didn't hang around whilst taking this image, the high wind making it bitterly cold.

Looking west along Wensleydale to Abbotside Common.

The River Ure
meanders along
central Wensleydale
overlooked by
Abbotside Common.

After a successful day along Wensleydale I couldn't resist stopping on the way home to take a picture of this frozen fell pony looking for food with the Howgill Fells in the background.

After days of being snowed out I was at last able to gain access to Swaledale from the east starting with the village of Grinton overlooked by Calver Hill.

St Andrew's Church in Grinton, Swaledale.

Sunlight reflects off the River Swale near Reeth.

Looking west along Swaledale.

The array of hay meadows and field barns around Gunnerside Bottoms in Swaledale with their neat lines, are arguably the most iconic in the whole of the Dales.

Lonely farmstead above Gunnerside, Swaledale.

With no sun to warm the air the village of Gunnerside in Swaledale looks very bleak – in stark contrast to the view in summer with green fields and bright sunlit skies.

Swaledale's Muker Meadows overlooked by Kisdon Scar.

Looking east along Swaledale across the Muker Meadows.

Bare tree at Muker.

Muker has been an important settlement for centuries, its relative prosperity being built on agriculture, lead mining and knitting. Hand knitting was a commercial industry in the village in the mid nineteenth century and the village is still known for its knitwear available from Swaledale Woollens. Muker Hay Meadows are of international importance with their rich variety of meadow flowers in the early summer.

Swaledale Sheep at Muker.

With the unrelenting cold the Swale starts to freeze at Wain Wath Force.

Icicles form at Wain Wath Force.

Snow drifts against a gatepost near Ribblehead Viaduct.

Ingleborough from the slopes above Ingleton.

Ingleborough, the second of the Yorkshire Three Peaks, towers above the village of Ingleton and dominates the scene from the busy A65 between Kendal and Skipton. Standing at 2372 feet (723m) Ingleborough is the most shapely of the Three Peaks and fills the area to the east of the B6255 between Ingleton and Ribblehead.

Whernside, the highest of the Three Peaks at 2415 feet (736m), from near Ribblehead Viaduct.

Looking into the sun above Ingleborough from the roadside above Chapel-le-Dale.

Snow-filled Shake holes adjacent to Ribblehead Viaduct.

Ribblehead Viaduct.

That was the end of the road for me on the back road out of Settle.

Snow drifts build up against the walls which enclose the narrow High Hill Lane above Settle.

Highland Cattle in the Yorkshire Dales? Yes, it's true – a herd of Highland Cattle just suited to the wintry conditions on High Hill above Settle.

Frozen locks on the Leeds and Liverpool Canal at Gargrave.

The Leeds and Liverpool Canal is the longest canal in Northern England at 127 miles long. It passes through 91 locks. Built over a 46 year period between 1770 and 1816 the canal prospered through the nineteenth century and was used for carrying stone, coal and many other goods.

The spectacular limestone cliffs of Gordale Scar near Malham.

Gordale Beck overlooked
by limestone outcrops at
Goredale Scar.

Janet's Foss is a popular waterfall
adjacent to Goredale Bridge
above Malham.

Steam train leaving Bolton Abbey Station on the Embsay and Bolton Abbey Steam Railway.

The sun sets over the frozen ruins of Bolton Abbey.

Snow-covered trees beside the River Wharfe at Bolton Abbey.

Every year around Christmas multi-coloured flood-lights illuminate the main buildings on the Bolton Abbey Estate. Just after dusk the lights spectacularly bring the structures to life against the darkening night sky. With the addition of snow on the ground the scene is transformed into a 'Faerieland'.

Above: Coloured light illuminates the dome on the Cavendish Memorial at Bolton Abbey.

Top: Floodlit ruins of Bolton Abbey Priory.

Left: Floodlights illuminate The Priory Church of St Mary and St Cuthbert, Bolton Abbey.

Lonely sheep enclosure high on Birkdale Common close to the source of the Swale.

The confluence of Whitsundale Beck and the Swale on a fearfully cold morning. With -10'C showing on the thermometer, waiting around outside with the camera on a tripod for the light to improve tested my outdoor clothing to the extreme!

Upper Swaledale early on the same bitterly-cold winter's morning

The snow may have cleared but I couldn't resist another set of images of the barns and pastures at Gunnerside Bottoms, Swaledale.

Close up of the morning frost on one of the field barns at Gunnerside Bottoms, Swaledale.

Snow lingers around Surrender Smelt Mill, high on the moors above Swaledale. Built in 1839 the mill operated for barely 40 years, smelting the lead ore from the local mines. The mill ran four hearths, three for ore and one for slag. The long flue climbs the hillside behind the mill.

Above: Icicles growing up the grasses alongside Cogden Gill.

Left: The adjacent Surrender Bridge over Mill Gill Beck.

Cogden Gill flows past the restored Grinton Smelt Mill. The buildings date from around 1820, although lead had been mined and processed on the site for at least the previous six centuries. The mill was last used for smelting lead in 1886. The two furnaces were originally water powered by a 7m diameter waterwheel in the diverted water-course.

Looking along the flue at Grinton Smelt Mill. The flue from the mill goes straight up Sharrow Hill where a triple-arched lime kiln can be found.

Possibly the most photographed barn in Swaledale, between Thwaite and Keld looking east down the dale.

Pair of field barns on Cloggerby Rigg overlooked by Kisdon, Upper Swaledale.

Looking across to Kisdon from Angram, Upper Swaledale.

The snow returns to Wensleydale in February.

Looking down onto Hawes from Sedbusk.

Left: Sheep hoping for a feed from the author near Hawes, Wensleydale.

Below: "That's better" – farmer feeding sheep at Sedbusk.

Opposite: "Are you looking at me?" – tup at Mile House Farm, Sedbusk.

Cam High Road above Bainbridge – this Roman road in true fashion runs almost straight as a die from the Virosidvm fort at Bainbridge all the way to Ingleton.

St Oswald's Church, Askrigg.

Countersett Quaker Meeting House. There is a long tradition of Quakerism in Wensleydale dating to the early visits of George Fox in the 1650s. Countersett Meeting House was first built in 1710 with subsequent improvements in 1772 and remains unchanged since then.

The sun glints off a partially frozen Semer Water.

A light dusting of snow lingers on the top of Addlebrough,
with the infant River Bain in the valley bottom.

Frozen Semer Water overlooked by Green Scar.

The thaw starts – snow banks cling to Kidstone Scar, in Bishopdale between Wensleydale and Wharfedale.

Meltwater fills Cray Gill and makes a spectacular sight as it pours over a limestone cove at Cray High Bridge above Wharfedale. In the summer these falls are frequently completely dry.

Pockets of snow surround a field barn at Cray.

I noticed this barn just over the wall and parked at Cray. Passing
through a gate into the fields I was enchanted by the fast flowing
water in Cray Gill in the foreground which was unseen from the road.

Limestone scars above Hubberholme, Wharfedale.

A bleak scene: clouds gather over the sunlit hillside above Cray with wind-blasted trees.

Late winter sunshine on Kettlewell, Wharfedale whilst the snow lingers on Great Whernside.

Afternoon sun on the Wharfe between Kettlewell and Starbotton.

Bridge over the Wharfe at Yockenthwaite.

Blue skies over the Wharfe along Langstrothdale.

I just managed to get this one image before the light went. Clouds brood
over the Wharfe at Deepdale Bridge along Langstrothdale.
I'm torn between this image and the one on Pages 122 &123
as to which is my favourite in the whole collection.

After my day in Wharfedale this barn in the valley of Sleddale caught my eye as I was driving back over the top on the way to Hawes.

Gayle Beck joins the River Ure near Hawes.

Green fields emerge – looking east along Wensleydale, from the same viewpoint as the snow-covered scene on pages 42 & 43.

The River Ure full of melt water flows over the ever popular Aysgarth Middle Falls beside Freeholders Wood, Wensleydale. The falls have attracted visitors for over 200 years including the poet William Wordsworth and his new wife Mary, who visited the day after their marriage in 1802.

The falls out of the back of the picturesque village of West Burton, Bishopdale. The falls are easily found from the village green but I wouldn't advise trying to get too close on the rocks to the right of the falls – I took a nasty tumble on the slippy surface ending up with a wet backside! However I am happy to report that no cameras were hurt in the making of this image.

Semer Water and the River Bain overlooked by Green Scar from Carpley Green Road. The tranquillity of this scene belies the howling and bitingly cold wind that was blowing, forcing me back to the protection of the car whilst waiting for the clouds to clear.

New born lambs herald the start of spring after the long winter months.

Spring sunshine on Haylands Bridge over the River Ure near Hawes.

Muker Literary Institute, Swaledale. The Literary Institute was built by public subscription in 1867
and originally contained a large library, a reading room with newspapers and a meeting room.

The River Swale gently flows beneath Ivelet Bridge near Muker.

Daffodils beside Malham Beck in the middle of Malham.